SUDDEN LIGHT

ENDA WYLEY

DEDALUS PRESS

Contents

~

Sudden Light / 11
Charging / 12
Photo in a Park / 14
Interviewing a Poet / 15
Indigo Bird / 16
Two Poems After the Painter Luca Signorelli:
Annunciation / 17
Lamentation at the Foot of the Cross / 18
All Souls' Day / 20
Omen / 21
Henry Shefflin / 22
Embrace / 23
Summerhill House, County Meath / 24
Death of an Archivist / 25
Visitor / 26
Happiness / 27
Great Big Bed / 30
Hand / 32
Above the River / 33
Follower / 34
Platform 1 East / 35
Lunch Blessing / 36
All the Dead / 37
Wedding, Late August / 39
Daphne Becomes a Tree / 41
May Ballet Performance / 42
Pumpkins, Waterloo Road / 43
Student / 44
Elegy for a Student / 45

Studio / 46

After a Fall / 48

Eyrie / 49

Impossible / Possible / 50

Empathy / 52

Girl in a Window / 53

Touch / 54

Through the Window / 55

Photos of My Mother / 56

Route 140 / 63

Back Then / 64

Light / 65

Visiting / 67

Notes and Acknowledgements / 70

for Freya & Peter Sirr

Li-Ti's Advice

If you own two coppers, said Li Ti on a journey,
buy one loaf of bread and one blossom.
The bread is there to fill you,
the blossom you buy is to tell you
that life is worth the living.

—Harry Martinson, from *Gräsen i Thule*, 1958,
translated by Stephen Klass.

Sudden Light

after Adam Zagajewski

So much has come my way –
the postman drops the artist's gift,

an ink sketch upright in my letter box.
What's there? His own mother's hands

cradling a green bowl, her face buried
deep inside: tender hunger, her last meal.

Later, the sun's a found ball our dog chases
across the Iveagh Gardens' sunken lawn, over

the grassy hump of the disused air-raid shelter
in Merrion Square. And there, the two bronze

lions' heads burst magic from Rutland Fountain –
water into this day's conch shell, for too long dry.

Summer will come. Like that one, years ago,
my mother told me all about, her fist of coins

ready to clink into the meter of the dark church
in Rome. Late afternoon, in the middle of her life,

but how the light came on for just a few minutes
and she saw in San Luigi dei Francesi those three

Caravaggios – reminding her of the poet's words:
They live in semi-darkness and suddenly there's light.

Charging

for Dermot Bolger
& in memory of Michael Hartnett

Before the light goes out
on this phone, before
the scramble for a plug
and the battery charges,
before the blind is rolled up
and the light angles
its way into my room –
before all this,
for these fading minutes
let me listen and watch.

In the clip you're sitting
in your tweed suit
complete with waistcoat
to honour your friend,
his poems in hand,
remembering
a morning he called
from a phone box
on Leeson Street.
He presses button A.
A joke. A new poem
before the line dies,
his money spent.

Oh, Angela Liston.
Oh, father that he kissed
for the last and first time.
Oh, woman that he loved
from the moment she died.

I hear it all now. The past opens
its pages, unearths him, stick cut
from a tree in Coole Park guiding
him home to Dartmouth Square.
My phone dies. The day charges.

Photo in a Park

What I think of now is not the photograph
but who took it. Who stood there with their back
to the fountain and kindly captured us, a young couple,
their six-week-old baby, a rug laid out on the grass?

Who was it that stopped casually on the gravel, saved us
like this in time? There'd been no sleep. I'd run through
the night like an innocent new athlete. To persist, endure,
to nurse in the depths of dark, the rest of the house asleep.

And yet, exhaustion was defeated by joy. Our little girl
all moon-eyed curiosity at everything that rustled, moved.
We sat on that rug so naturally, at ease together, my legs
folded sideways, you with the paper open in the sunshine.

Zoom in now and check the date. It is June, many years ago.
We are brave first-time parents marking a patch for ourselves
in the summer park – and that stranger, man who catches us here,
what does he do? Leaves us to what will come our way. Moves on.

Interviewing a Poet

for Eiléan Ní Chuilleanáin

The cameraman pausing, head back:
then counting down three … two …
Inhale, start again and all comes right,
the poem lifting your dead mother up.

Huge tree of the cupola, the virgin
spiralling towards mist, towards shining –
hands that are love passing her through them.
Such care, the afternoon suddenly changed.

This is what matters, the questions
flung aside, the body leant forward
listening to your poem that makes
something happen beyond explanation.

A mystery that is light in this room. The city
sirens coming closer, demanding that we leave.
Not now, too much is here, your head bowed
over the page, your fair hair brushing its edges.

I see you lifting the words, your face shifting
with the weight of them all: then they come to
the high edge of their cloud and we are spent,
return to our lives dazed and the camera stops.

Indigo Bird

in memory of Janet Mullarney

After her death, the artist rises
from the kitchen floor, surveys

the indigo bird she's cut in lino,
wipes her hands on a cloth and sees

from her window that spring has come,
is a patch of park with cherry blossom.

Then her peacock struts through the hall,
flapping out into the stilled world

ahead into time, to here, where we stand now
at her house with the narrow white door –

on the gate our candle flickering upright
in amber memory. She watches all this –

how we walk back through the dark,
our neighbourhood subdued.

There's a cat, white on a shabby wall.
Cranes reach their long arms

to the moon's pink aura. All of this
she sees, minutes after she dies.

And how in Newmarket, graffiti startles
on night's billboard: *Try Poetry.*

Annunciation

Such haste: the angel racing in
from the side of the frame.
He has entered the picture
with purpose. I have news
and it imbues me with gravity.
Do not brush me aside, he says.

Wind of his wings, a billow
of ruby gown – his auburn hair
swept back and I imagine
a peacock feather plaited there,
a dazzling blue that stops
the woman in her tracks.

The seed of surprise is already
settled deep inside of her,
a mystery she must accept,
she who has slept as a virgin
until now, her face cooled
by the wall she pressed her
young face to every night.

And yet she knew this day
would come, this rustling
of godly power, her chamber
lit with her future and she
willing to do what is asked
of her – go the distance.

after Luca Signorelli, 1441–1523, Cortona, Italy

Lamentation at the Foot of the Cross

Any minute now, the lady in the gallery
with the dog will let him go and he'll be off,
madly diving into the painting – such havoc!

The man on the ladder is wobbling,
curses him. Already such a job to pull
from the dead man's wrists those nails –

such wailing below over his lifeless
body – and now, this dog turning
the head of the bereft mother.

Briefly, she takes it in with her deep
and sorrowful eyes – the yapping
creature – then returns to her grief.

What now? The dog could go off
with the painter to his two villas
high up in the hills of Cortona.

They're the payment for his work,
I've heard. But the dog is wiser,
leaps back into his own world

where his mistress waits, carries him –
her long, pale arms – to the balcony
in the heat of their shared afternoon.

It is better that the dog does this –
look out onto the town's red roofs,
than suffer the axe of the ignorant

back there, where they break up
the altarpiece for florins, its fragments
sent from Matelica, far around the world.

after Luca Signorelli, 1441–1523, Cortona, Italy

All Souls' Day

for Paula Meehan

All of them are on the way back –
an old photo found, a certain smell
or the touch of a particular material,
something someone says and they're
here again. Bewildering ink spreads
on a starched white collar, dark drops
on blotting paper from a phantom pen.

Knock on a door. Who's there? Nobody.
Mark of a hand pressed on winter glass
seen for a second, then vanished. The heart
quickens, pulse skitters with each unseen
weight across floorboards in the room above
where no baby lies and yet the cries thicken
the night, a cradle rocks that's no longer there.

All of this a reminder. Before we follow on
to where we hope they are – welcoming us
as the friends we knew and loved and lost –
to strike a match in the dark for them.
It is November. Candlelight warms this kitchen table.
Here, the wind of their return is trembling at my door.
Let me in, they call. I have no fear and do as they ask.

Omen

It was our dog's growl that sent me to the door.
Late August and a mist had come, veil of grey
and damp making invisible the streets of Blackpitts.

Not Lord Roper's ghost riding headless on his eternal
mare from his orchards into the city's heart,
but another unearthly creature – its pale ears erect,

its body shaved by a brutal sickness, robbed
of all its rich fur – that shot out, a flare of russet,
then hid under night cars, fearful of human chatter.

Mange of its older years and only bitterness left –
that it has come to this! – defeated aura enveloping it.
I stand in a pool of front door light, and it is not afraid.

Stops. Stares back at me. It is red-eyed, ashamed
but wanting me to see. Its tail long and thin, ending
sharply as its life surely will. *This is what I have become.*

Henry Shefflin

Portrait by Gerry Davis, The National Gallery of Ireland

And who would not want to be
Henry Shefflin, turned from home,
standing straight-backed, head high,

his feet firmly apart on the Ballyhale pitch,
a hurley swung over his shoulder, the other
hand casual in his trouser pocket?

No muddied shorts and jersey now –
he is king of these grounds, the suited monarch
of all about him, facing the steely-eyed future,

his past a sliotar struck far across the field.
Centre of all things, now he likes to stare up
the elegant stairs to Canova's 'Amorino',

and is older than this marble prince, though
no less determined, both with hands raised –
one to a bow, the other to the hurley's handle.

Embrace

The National Gallery of Ireland

They squint at canvases, are greedy –
Tangier, the white city, Fontainebleau
sun, the blinding light of Palm Springs –

they want it all. To lounge with the languid
sunbathers on their cushions, to be cooled
by the shadow of John Lavery's umbrella.

But the man by the rowers at Grez stops
so suddenly in the middle of the gallery
that I wonder what exactly it is he wants.

Such a lonely figure he cuts too, dazed
among the punters who brazenly
obstruct each other's view –

when out of the blue he flings his arms open,
and from a bench comes a woman of feline grace.
I might be the only one who sees them embrace.

But then there's the painter with his young daughter
reclining in their own framed affection. How knowingly
they gaze at this sudden love in a hot and teeming room.

Summerhill House, County Meath

for Lynda Mulvin & in memory of Niall McCullough

What I like is this: walking up the avenue
with you – the ancient trees all about us,
the expectation of gravel under our boots,
and the ghost of a lost house expanding
up ahead across the October horizon.

Not even the fawn bull whose land
it is now can frighten us into retreat,
can stop us from lifting the rusting gate,
our city coats marked by its iron bars.
We're on a mission, are busy imagining

gate lodges like pineapples built here once,
sunken gardens and the grassy hill's sundial,
the lofty hall, the dining room and covered ceilings,
then the rage that burnt all of this in 1921.
Ireland's most beautiful house gone!

And the wind, I like this too: think of it now,
wild as the empress who came here from Austria
to secretly hunt, and who rode up this avenue –
carefree, whip in hand tight as her beauty –
years before an assassin shot her dead.

Death of an Archivist

The city cannot know you're gone.
It is too busy.

It has its own light to care for.
How it must uncover what is and isn't there.

And yet it needed you while you were here.
How else could it have made sense of itself, or we of it?

But nothing is lost that cannot be retrieved.
So much comes back and claims the page.

No one is ever gone whose name is said,
whose life, like yours, is recalled.

Visitor

after the painting by James Hanley

For now, the man is happy like this,
poised in the deep blue sky above the city,
lying face down, his knees bent, his feet

kicked back, arms spread, his skin burnt
from the sun, his fingers open to what
will come to him any second now.

Below him, a plume of smoke is dusting
the colonnades, hides from view the tower
and its bell that will ring when he falls.

And when he does, the four figures standing
upright above the portico will raise their holy
hands in prayer, in loss – for not even they

or the angel on top of the dome can save him.
But first, there's the church spires to admire,
the silhouette of a plane and a proud horseman

to wonder at, before string is a worry caught
in his hand, before quayside spectators look up,
startled and ask, *Who is this man, this visitor?*

For a moment, he is happy just like this,
suspended in the sky's elation. Then the city
exhales, and the man, weightless no more, falls.

Happiness

in memory of Mary Lavin

You're making this old crock shake.
Like a bird on the hover dipping a wing,

you drop one shoulder, twist the handlebars,
turn at last into a quiet triangular place –

this park you've been on a mission to reach.
Inside its railings the great trees are ready.

They spread their branches, filter light
onto the sculptor's shiny silver curves.

*Please refrain from touching
or climbing on this …*

So, dip the other wing, and swing
through the gates, brake to a halt.

Glitter of the slowing spokes, you dismount
from joy, crunch past the fountain and out

towards Lad Lane. Look right, she's there,
standing behind the office's tall glass, staring

at you with those same half-smiling eyes
that met the camera's gaze decades ago.

This photo I've cycled here to view.
Writer who knew all about bicycles.

The widow's son racing down the hill,
wind in his hair, scholarship in his heart,

who swerves, flies over handlebars
to an early death. *Why did he put*

the price of an old clucking hen
above the price of his own life?

Writer caught in black and white,
her arms flung across the mantlepiece,

the rough mews wall her backdrop.
Handknit cardigan her warmth,

tweed skirt her practical garb.
But the medallion is a giveaway.

Artful round sun that circles
back to now –

to this ancient light,
to the bicycle flung aside,

the coach house door
opening to reveal her.

She's thrown coffee beans
on the hob minutes before,

filling the dining room air
with a whiff of elsewhere.

Piazza Navona,
Boulevard Saint-Michel …

She pulls the pins from her messy
bun, lets her long grey hair down.

The pendant light swings above, wine
flows and the table is forever round.

Great Big Bed

*'For one night only
naked in your arms.'*
—Beatriz, Countess of Dia, c. 1175

This great big bed
makes me think of you.
Not that I've ever lain
a full long night
with you
but if I could,
it would be here,
would be now,
in this great big bed,
the skylight overhead.

Slant of hail,
a blind of snow,
the whole world
silent outside
and us within
breathless
in a storm of sheets –
the high triple mattress
a royal test of love.

But look, a small crack
in the glass
where the weather
sneaks in –
oh, cruel observer
of what we're about! –

sleet to freeze our eyelids,
wind's bitter slicing
of our cheeks.

And then –
so slowly –
how a single flake
of snow
can drop
into your mouth
and melt
upon your tongue
that is busy
in its own way
melting over mine.

Hand

It was a short cut,
so we took the fairy path,
over the fields
all those years ago,
after the pub closed –
a group of us laughing
and not afraid until the night
claimed us and we were lost,
boulders fierce around us,
bushes prickling our arms,
our footing uncertain
in the soft soil.

Then, the others far ahead,
I felt your hand in mine –
warm life unexpected there
as you guided me
towards distant voices,
though we did not want
to reach them,
were happy just touching,
our fingers tight in each other's.

There were no rings,
no children, no futures –
until we heard,
Look! It's this way!
and we saw
the house lights ahead,
stumbled through trees,
pulled our hands apart.

Above the River

I'm across a busy street watching you,
the cathedral's shadow hiding me from view.
You are slipping into your old apartment building.

A goose feather duvet you've just bought is all ready
for you to unroll on top of your futon, soon to be ours.
But first, you've plans: throw out your cigarettes for me,

paint over the smoke stains on the ceiling above your chair.
Lay fresh lino on the bathroom floor, a startling cobalt blue –
blue as the ache of light on the sheet of glass we'll heave

days later up Clanbrassil Street – such agony! – mad notion
of ours to make a new-fangled table on the waiting trestle.
But not yet those first meals, not yet their tang–

lemony garlic, olives scooped from the market stall
into our yearning hands. Not yet our early laying down.
Not yet the young oranges unpeeled, fresh on our skin –

not yet our love, mysterious as the roof garden. Not yet
any of that. Just this – to stand above the river at the edge
of Lord Edward Street and see you again as you were then.

And I want to shout: Wait! Wait! Look back at me weaving
my way across to you. Look back. But the night gathers up,
scatters onto the pavement our fierce history…

Follower

See me, standing at the bright
graffitied wall: *U Are Alive.*
And look up to the man
leaning out his attic window.
He's painting his sill white
for you to net on your phone.

Click. Later, in the Iveagh Gardens,
frost is white dust on the statues.
A dog on the sunken lawn growls
at elephant bones buried below
by the zoo in nineteen twenty-two.

Further east, snow on the maze
swirls its way to the inner sundial.
I would chase you there, if I could –
find you as a small child again,
in the gaze of the boating tower.
But I slip on ice, grasp a railing,

steady myself, then set off again
in your wake. You're so far ahead –
how straight-backed, effortlessly,
you possess the day – and I call out,
but you don't turn, don't hear me.
So, I stumble on, following you.

Platform 1 East

Before the sweat and bustle
the long stretch of platforms –
us dragging our life on wheels
to a small train heading inland –
let us whoosh upwards in a lift
to the top of this old building,
stand amongst the roof terrace's
terracotta pots and gaze over
at the ribbed slates and domes.

Let's look down
to our time together last night.
The underground restaurant,
the twirl of spaghetti.
tomato sauce staining our shirts,
and, after, the scarred men
in a circle of drugs, whistling

at you, our daughter oblivious.
A single leaping rat guided us
through shadowy laneways
to our airless, shuttered room.
One last look. Platform 1 East
waiting, the engine raring to go,
to take us north of Rome, away
from all this noise and grime,
from all of this relentless beauty.

Lunch Blessing

for Fernando Trilli

Two lizards speed away
at the sound of our feet.
Trays of aubergines –
their golden hearts –
olives, mozzarella,
all carried from over
the fields, from women
in the tiny market, to here.

A drip of oil, a string
of spaghetti spills onto
the scorching stones:
the Siamese cat pounces.
We sweat in the heat,
sweat with the meats,
our friendship abundant
as platters on this long table.

Later, three white butterflies
will lead us all the way up
to the old walled town.
But for now, breadcrumbs
fall like summer snow
on our check tablecloth
and the bells of Sant'Angelo
ring their blessings on us all.

All the Dead

All the dead behind us, pasted
on a billboard in vibrant colours,
so celebratory that I am mistaken,
think they're faces of opera singers.

I let the sun warm my face,
the wood of the chipped bench
heating my spine, imagine then
their voices soaring in the ghost air –

imagine the bells of St Francis
ring above us: the townsfolk
humming, their hips swaying
to this exultant spectral music.

Until it comes to me that
each name has defined dates
beneath it, each poster
a notice of a life gone –

displayed for all to see at the base
of the narrow, twisty street.
Our hearts pounding at the end
of our descent, beating for the loss

of those we never knew
in this hot and foreign town,
feeling for those who once
climbed where we just did,

stretched out their arms,
embraced the dizzying views,
and just for that moment forgetting
that their end would ever come at all.

Wedding, Late August

I.

All day the bells rang
from the church of the archangel.

All day the voices carried
high and laughing over the still, hot air.

All day joy unsettled our quiet lazing
in the sun, our dry and silent hours.

II.

And far off, glasses clinked, and music thumped
so loudly that not even the cicadas could be heard.

Later, at the bend of the road, the wooden church doors
were bolted, and we watched, leaning against

the high stone wall, saw a bonfire lit in the grounds
of the old villa, felt in the half-light that night

was slinking, like a Siamese cat along our backs.
And a great longing came to be with them all,

to walk barefoot down the rough, sun-yellowed
lane and to ask, *do you mind if we join you?*

III.

In the darkness that eventually came,
the bride's ecstasy rose pale as the daunting moon

over the cypress trees, and we danced until dawn,
were renewed. And still the confetti remained

white and heart-shaped, clustering at the flap
of the rusty gate, like blossoms from way back home.

IV.

It blows now beyond the church, up the lane, across
the glistening olive groves. It knots in the hair of guests,

lightens the green hedgerow, moves beyond everything
we saw and heard, spreads love in its own way

from the ands that threw it –
blessings flung on the newlyweds who have not

looked back at those heaps of white paper, such a part
of their big day, that the curate will soon try to sweep away.

Daphne Becomes a Tree

Apollo and Daphne (Bernini) 1622–1625,
Galleria Borghese, Rome

And does Daphne want to leap
from this dark room out onto
the garden's lemon trees below,
the city hers to go where she likes,
to do in it whatever she wants?

No, she has other things
to worry about. His hand
on her hip – such strength!
Rush of his drapes in chase.
Escape his relentless desire –

that's what she must do.
Hair a burst of change, hands
a twirl of twigs and leaves, feet
rooting a new freedom in the earth.
Her heart quivering under laurel bark.

May Ballet Performance

Late afternoon, the May heat
quenched by a slow fall of drizzle.
We walk to the market square,
climb stairs to a hall, its windows
framing an early summer rainbow.

Then young ballerinas dance –
our daughters in black leotards
on pink pointe shoes, all pale
and long-necked, their lips
pinched, hair tight under nets

and their arms like stems, fingers
delicately flowering at their tips.
Plié, arch, tap, tap,
now jump, jump, jump!
While outside the rain pours down,

washing the past into gutters
until the streets gleam
fresh as stall apples,
pips blown to the wind.

Pumpkins, Waterloo Road

Three long-haired children
cross-legged at the top
of their high steps –

bent in action, scraping out
pumpkins for candles. Orange
innards reckless on the granite.

Doric pillars on either side
salute them, framed as they are
below the whitewashed lintel.

No camera here to catch all this –
just my pen to scribble it down,
unheeded by them, this late afternoon.

Let darkness fall, let candles be lit
in these hard-won jagged eyes and grins –
pumpkins on a Dublin windowsill.

Student

for Brian Donnelly

Early morning
bike rides
up the long
college avenue,
farm dogs
barking at me, dewy
tarmac under trees.

Winter, spring
and summer term –
always that long
avenue leading
to formal red brick,
clusters of birds
and one morning
when I was eighteen,
news of the poet gone.

Then there were
only high windows –
mist reflected,
clearing into
a December day –
and choir songs
tumbling
out of them,
exultant, endless.

On the death of Philip Larkin

Elegy for a Student

in memory of Christa Vander Wyst, 2000–2024

You came from the back of Books Upstairs,
Ada Limón's *The Carrying* a gift from you
that last November day we met.

Poems of such ferocity on the jolting bus
to home. Old gate swung inward, key in the lock,
lights on. None of this will come to you again.

Evening fades into fox time, vixen cries down a street.
While we sleep, night is the thief rustling at the edge
of our dreams where you enter quietly, stay only a while.

Studio

for Niamh Clarke & Frances Ryan

But wait, ideas will come, like
this afternoon when you reach
a fork in the wood, sense there
a spectral tryst of two lovers

under dense trees. Breathe gently.
Do not disturb them. This still
moment allows you in and then
they vanish, and you walk on.

Love survives lightly and with
such delicacy, it surprises you.
Later, the door leads to a stair
and you clamber up to a room

where the wind can't reign
or distract you from your
intense and modest ways,
your intricate pencil offerings.

A book of Rilke's poems bent open,
words that make you reach for paper,
sketch yellow tulips that defeat gloom,
unexpected colour printed in this room.

Now a magnifying glass to peer at
the women's tiny faces, drawn by you.
They are longing for their men to return
from the war, their pain abundant

as the flowers they clutch, waiting.
Now, your table to lean over, get close
to the woman with her elbows bent,
shoulders hunched, her long fingers

hiding her face. No need to prise
her hands apart, find what's there
on her warm palms. Enough for us
to guess what is concealed –

her lifeline a path into another
forest, where branches encircle her,
renew her, then release her with care,
Your sketch pad once empty, filled at last.

After a Fall

The poet comes with long grey hair,
a used and much-loved book as a gift.
She comes with rain, the earth so dry,
the heat and smells of southern Italy.
She knows all about broken bones,
her husband had a way with falling
and she herself fell once, tripped into
the dark room they kept their wine in
and broke her nose. So much blood,
but little else to be concerned about –
the nose healed by itself, she said.

Then the sculptor comes with thin
chocolate biscuits, her long fingers
dark from welding in the foundry –
her clutch of dimpled bronze tern eggs,
to install on the grass by Baltray's shore,
and her cast iron starfish to cartwheel
playfully over Port Oriel's harbour wall.

We eat chickpeas, hunks of rough bread,
our stories scattering like breadcrumbs.
How love can find a new path into life,
the way an old house can be renewed,
its heart a stove, abundant rising heat,
its gate left open always for friends.

Into my kitchen you came –
your news, your vibrancy a mirror
held up to my life. And a thought –
that I could have again what I had
before, make of my days a purpose.

Eyrie

The world I know below me.
It knows me too, just hasn't seen me
for a while. And yet, I like to look at it

from my eyrie, high above the street.
And it is good, I think, to see that others
make of it their own –

young man belting up the hill, balances
his phone on the handlebars, two workmen
with their backs to me, paint up and down

on the opposite wall a mint green canvas.
Come night, the stealthy graffiti artists
splay their vision there. *Beako!*

The sign that always brought a smile,
Happy's News and Booze, and up here
lavender oil steams the air, spills out.

A child below sniffs my potion,
turns his face upwards, sees mine
pressed to the windowpane.

Sprite of my younger self, bursting
from the school gates to home.
I rise from pain into the gloom of day.

All I see below will soon welcome me back –
my once fractured life healing,
following the light steps of a child.

Impossible / Possible

Impossible to open the can,
to cut the thick loaf of bread,
to squeeze the toothpaste out.

Impossible to negotiate the shower,
to climb the steep, narrow stairs –
slowly up, so slowly down.

The envelope is too tricky
to slit open, a jagged smile
your own mouth can't make.

Impossible a pair of socks.
Press your big toe in first,
stretch your good arm

to yank it on, then try
the other twitching foot.
And to feel joy is near

impossible, until the opiate
numbs the pain and sun filters
from the tops of chimneys

from the far away blue
of the Dublin mountains
into your small room.

The white of the walls
illuminates
with possibilities.

The world is no longer
shuffled into. There was never
the crack of a shoulder and wrist

on violent pavement, never
the January cold, persistent
as an approaching ambulance.

Empathy

is a long garden
stretching
into the morning.

It is wild and responsive,
knows you want only to leave
the house's gloom and stand

in green stillness: it is
a slow kindness
that seeps through you.

Morning dew quenches
the thirst of plants and relief
will come, firm as a fallen

pear in your palm. Lift it up
this fruit from the tangled grass,
smell in its skin the sweet

benevolence that found you
in this old room where you
least expected to be.

for Dr Mark Murphy

Girl in a Window

Your blind pops up like an eyelid.
There's a flash of recognition
and I know you are back again,
at the window that's diagonal
from mine, across the quiet street.

You push a curtain aside, balance
on your bed close to the glass,
inhale and flick your cigarette
onto the ledge. You spot me,
slanted on pillows. What am I doing here?

Do you wonder why days go by
and I lie here inert, heavy as cement?
If I could, I would draw a lock of your hair
back from your face, ask you to walk
wide-eyed through the streets with me.

Touch

And then there is the secret world,
the one where I say, touch can confuse
the brain that has empowered itself
through my pain. So, surprise it –
touch me and let endorphins startle
my neural pathways. Let flexibility
become a meadow of soft happenings.
See, you touch, and everything is possible.
Who'd have thought it could be so easy?

Through the Window

Newtown Park House, Blackrock, Co. Dublin: 11th April 2020

Odd but necessary the solution that comes to us,
to stare through glass at you: your parched face
slanted towards the afternoon light. On your wall
a forest you'd painted when we were young.

Two red-coated figures walk under trees
and we remember the bedtime story you read us –
wardrobe portal into snow, a lamppost, Narnia's wood.
Now, here is the masked carer, opening the window

to the love we yell in – such force it unsettles you.
We're ready to turn back to our strange world
where we stand apart, can't touch, but lucky
we've seen your lips pucker into one last kiss.

Photos of My Mother

1.

You, standing on a large
kitchen colander, painted white
in a school hall. Ten years old
and the nuns have put you there –
long, long curls rolling down
to your shoulders, your hands
pressed in prayer, a halo of stars
over your head. The Assumption,
and you've been chosen to ascend
to heaven with your angelic face.

'Yes. I was a great little actress.
But after that I cut my hair short.
Got myself a pair of scissors
and chopped away. Your granny
was horrified but I didn't want
to be Mary ever again. I wanted
to be young, wanted to be modern.'

2.

You in a white shirt, wide belt
and colourful skirt, all of them
stolen from your sister. Your first
dance with my father. His hand
tight around your tiny waist.
Your face is radiant with love.
'You took my shirt without
asking!' Your sister's fury.
'I'm locking that wardrobe door
and I'm keeping the key!'

3.

You on a daytrip. A beach
in Crosshaven. You sit on dad's
raincoat, your nose nuzzling
his. You're just eighteen.
'I won't allow you to marry
until you're twenty-one!'
your father warns. You are
his youngest and he never
wants you to go, can't bear
the thought of it. Eventually
you leave for your honeymoon,
and he is full of such sorrow
after the wedding breakfast
that he hangs his head, says
to his wife and your older sister,
'Well, 'tis easy counting us now.'

4.

Gathered at Kent station, Cork.
Your parents and sister crying.
You're moving to Dublin
to start your married life.
1960s Ireland
and it may as well be
Australia
you're heading to.
'Why would anyone
leave Cork for Dublin?
I mean to say, haven't we
everything we need here, girl?'
Your parents perplexed, bereft
and you're sad for them –
but excited all at once.

Freedom is a basement flat
on Palmerston Road.
Your own front door!
Freedom is a ragged carpet
to roll back and find the gift
of oak floors underneath.
Ignore the mean landlord
berating you, threats
to increase your rent
for defiling his flat.
Instead, polish those wide
magnificent floors. See,
your future shining there.

5.

You, photographed
coming over O'Connell Bridge,
one arm around my father,
In the crook of the other a parcel.
'What were you carrying, mum?'
'A pound of grass seed
for our first house.
And Bertrand Russell's
A History of Western Philosophy,
a birthday present for your father.'
The camera clicks.
The street photographer is paid.
Your first child twitches inside of you.
My older brother. A honeymoon baby.

6.

You, free and young.
The sun on your face,
the wind in you dark curls.
You stand on a rock
in white shorts
and a sleeveless shirt,
welcoming
what will be.
Your right hand
lets flow in the breeze
a silk scarf that is
as exuberant as you are.

For months after your death,
I face this photo outwards
on the windowsill.
The postman, neighbours,
friends, all comment
on your loveliness.
But the sun is harsh,
begins to fade your features
and I turn you inwards
to me, to privacy.
You're this small photo
on my desk now.
I thumb the dust away,
search in your face
for mine, whisper,
'Mother, where are you now?'

7.

You are forever kneeling
at our gate, your arms
stretched out to me,
racing home from school.
I am three years old and you
gather me close to you, the ring
on your finger glinting with love.
This last picture forever with me,
before the album closes.

Route 140

takes me to your hands – the blue, fine
veins of them – your engagement ring
and wedding band loose now.

Those rings that you always left
on the kitchen sill after our noisy
dinners. Route 140 takes me

to your face, paper thin, yellowing,
your eyes childlike when you
catch sight of my father,

your fingers unfurling
to hold his hand, your mouth near
to his ear: *I depend on you.*

Back Then

She was tempted, nearly left
with those people, who'd rowed up
and beached on the white of her
hospital bed. But we were small,
only children, and she was still
young – a mother who said,
No. I'm cold. I must go back.

And so, her fever lapped away
left with their boats that bobbed
way out to that unknown place.
And we were saved back then
and she was ours again
for four strong decades more.

But tonight, she's had enough.
Though the nurse's hands are kind,
our mother pinches her parched lips
against pain. She is waiting for them
who will come in beauty, come in sun.
And this time she will say, *yes.*

Light

And how on mornings like this
she must have walked the empty
house on her own, all of us gone
to school – a light just like this
finding its way into the hall,
through the pale devilled glass
onto the swirling '70s carpet.

Light that I see again now, making
the brown couch look more tattered
from all our loud shenanigans on it –
cushion fights, whoops – sliding down
its defeated back into our teenage years.

In our country, she is not allowed
to work after she marries, not the way
my father does, a packed train to the city
and home each day at five: and yet
her work is here – morning light
that she embraces on her own
in this silent home of ours.

Home that I have never really left.
The hall table, the heavy black
phone, the wooden banister slide,
raucous games in the long garden.
I go back there now, take her hands
in mine, am a ghost come from my
future, back to her past. Then what?

The house to clean, the dinner
to be cooked by her for us later.
But first, this lying down with her,
just for a moment on her big bed.
The light that falls on us both now,
our fingers touching in this other
world where I am with her again.

Visiting

after a photograph by Amelia Stein

We come in to this – dark shutters
weathered by time, folded back,
the sudden light a gift.

An urge to lean over
the wrought-iron railing,
pluck pale leaves

from the summer tree
to cool our flushed faces.
The journey too long,

the carriages jolting,
our hands clammy.
But first, this –

new room that welcomes,
gathers us into the still
relief of its afternoon.

We want to claim not just
its light, but the shadows
brushed finely on the wall –

a secret world
of shifting grey lines, a reflection
of another room we could never enter,

until now. Drowsy, we sink
into the hush of this waiting space,
room within room, its mystery a veil

drawn aside, revealing what was always
there – a voice unheard, a door left ajar,
waiting for us to step inside, arrive.

Notes and Acknowledgements

The poem 'Lamentation at the Foot of the Cross' was inspired by the Matelica Altarpiece, painted by Luca Signorelli in 1504–1505 for the church of Sant'Agostino in Matelica, central Italy. Signorelli was paid the considerable sum, at the time, of 105 florins for his work, with which he was able to buy two houses in his city. The large panel was dismembered and dispersed around the world in the mid-eighteenth century. 'Man on a Ladder,' is one of six known fragments of this altarpiece. The surviving fragments today are currently housed in museums and collections around the world, including the Museo Civico, Bologna, the National Gallery of Art, Washington D.C, and private collections in Genoa, Rome and England.

The poem 'Happiness' was inspired by Mary Lavin, 1912–1996, one of the most celebrated writers of her generation and a master of the short story. The lines in my poem, 'Why did he put / the price of an old clucking hen / above the price of his own life?' is a quote from Mary Lavin's short story, 'The Widow's Son'. Mary Lavin Place, a cultural initiative by IPUT, Real Estate Dublin, is the first public space in Ireland to be named after a woman writer. It links Wilton Place to Lad Lane in Dublin, where Mary Lavin lived and worked between 1958 and 1981. A portrait of Mary Lavin by the German photographer Evelyn Hofer, taken in the writer's mews, 1966, can be seen at Mary Lavin Place and a sculpture by Eilis O'Connell is in Wilton Park.

Acknowledgements are due to the following publications in which a number of these poems, or versions of them, originally appeared: *Where We Are Now,* ed. Carol Ann Duffy Manchester Metropolitan University (April 2020), *Poems from Pandemic,* Munster Literature Centre, (2020), *Moments,* 21 poems selected by Marion Molteno in response to the lockdown (January 2021), the trans-Atlantic journal *Trasna*, (2020), *The Irish Times, High Window, Local Wonders: Poems of our Immediate Surrounds,* ed. Pat Boran (Dedalus Press, 2021), *Southward*, Summer issue 42 summer, (2022), *Romance Options: Love Poems for Today*, ed. Leeanne Quinn & Joseph Woods (Dedalus Press, 2022), *Vital Signs: Poems of Illness and Healing*, ed. Martin Dyar (Poetry Ireland, 2022), *Eden is a Backyard, New Climate Poems From Word to Action*, ed. Cathy Wittmeyer (Edition Eupalinos, Liechtenstein, 2024), *Cyphers* issue 93, 96, 98 ed. Eiléan Ní Chuilleanáin, *Poetry Ireland Review* 140, ed. Annmarie Ní Churreáin. Featured poet, *New Hibernian Review,* University of St Thomas, St Paul, MN, U.S.A 2024.

The following poems were broadcast on the cited programmes: 'Through the Window' was broadcast on *The Poetry Programme* Pandemic Special, RTÉ Radio 1, June 2020. The poems 'Annunciation' and 'Embrace' were broadcast on *Sunday Miscellany,* RTÉ Radio 1, December 2023. The following poems, or versions of them, 'Lunch Blessing,' 'Platform 1, East,' 'Photos of My Mother' and 'Photo in a Park', were broadcast on *Sunday Miscellany,* RTÉ Radio 1, 2024. The poem 'Henry Shefflin' was displayed nationally on Irish Rail commuter services, in railway stations and in public libraries as part of Poetry Ireland's 'Good Sports' themed promotion for Poetry Day Ireland, 2024.

I am indebted to the following two people without whom this book could not have been written: Peter and Freya Sirr. To Pat Boran and Raffaela Tranchino at Dedalus Press, much gratitude. For the great support that I received following a fall in January 2023, I want to thank Dr Mark Murphy, Lisa Branigan my physiotherapist, and Dr Gaafar, St James's Hospital. I also want to thank Niamh Hyland and Nick Kelly for an inspiring stay in Cortona, Italy. Thanks also to Amelia Stein for her wonderful photograph, to my father Jack Wyley and all my family, friends, and my aunt and namesake Enda Wyley.